THE JEWEL BOX GARDEN

Poppy —
Happy Planting!

Thomas Hobbs

THE JEWEL BOX GARDEN

THOMAS HOBBS

PHOTOGRAPHS BY DAVID McDONALD

Patty –
With Happy Memories
of Victoria !!
xx
Thomas Hobbs

RAINCOAST BOOKS

Vancouver

First published in 2004 by
Raincoast Books
9050 Shaughnessy Street
Vancouver, British Columbia
Canada   V6P 6E5
www.raincoast.com

Raincoast Books acknowledges the ongoing financial support of the Government of Canada
through The Canada Council for the Arts and the Book Publishing Industry Development Program
(BPIDP); and the Government of British Columbia through the BC Arts Council.

Edited by Scott Steedman
Interior Design by Stacey Noyes

NATIONAL LIBRARY OF CANADA CATALOGUING IN PUBLICATION
Hobbs, Thomas
          The jewel box garden / Thomas Hobbs.
Includes index.
ISBN 1-55192-601-6
1. Gardens—Design. I. Title.
SB472.45.H63 2004   712'.6   C2003-906479-4

Printed & Bound in Hong Kong by Book Art Inc., Toronto
10 9 8 7 6 5 4 3 2 1

PREVIOUS PAGE *A **Sempervivum** tableau by* DAVIS DOLBAK, *see page 26.*

"At long last I saw the door in the wall. I hadn't gone through it, but at least I saw it."

ALAN HELMS

CHAPTER 1	Life, As We Dream It Could Be	6
CHAPTER 2	Dream Big	20
CHAPTER 3	The Jewel Box	30
CHAPTER 4	Thinking Like A Plant	46
CHAPTER 5	It's All About Me	60
CHAPTER 6	Benefits Package	74
CHAPTER 7	Boogie Oogie Oogie	88
CHAPTER 8	Gilding The Lily	104
CHAPTER 9	Casa Triangulo	118
CHAPTER 10	Tastes Like Chicken	132
CHAPTER 11	Investment Potting	144
CHAPTER 12	Stirring Up Ghosts	162
	Index	176

CHAPTER I *Life, as we dream it could be*

NOTICE I DIDN'T SAY, "LIFE, AS WE DREAM IT IS," BUT AS IT could be. One of the few aspects of life we do have some control over is our gardens. Whether it is an outdoor terrace or balcony or a city plot, we can turn dreams into visions and visions into reality. All you need are patience, money (sad, but true) and commitment.

I prefer the word "commitment" to the word "work," because gardening isn't work when it's for yourself. Most people use gardening as therapy, to unwind after a busy day or a hectic week. By letting yourself get in contact with the earth, by dealing with plants instead of people, you will feel refreshed, calmed — and gratified because you're accomplishing something. As I putter about in the garden, I like to envision one current going out of me and a different current coming in. I deliberately try to connect to *something*, and that is why my garden stops traffic.

Try to create an oasis of beauty. The smaller your space, the easier this is going to be. Larger gardens need divisions to break them up, but I cannot stand the phrase "garden rooms" — it sounds too *planned*. I would rather experience a series of surprise visions, without walls. This could happen on a small terrace, or between two houses. It could be a well-placed water feature, followed by a collection of treasured potted ferns or succulents on a charming antique plant stand, approached on a pebble mosaic sidewalk.

PREVIOUS PAGE *In the* SEATTLE *garden of* GLENN WITHEY *and* CHARLES PRICE, *a few glass fishing floats in a copper dish create a simple water feature. Endlessly rearranged by the wind, they remind us that not all containers must hold plants.*

LEFT *In* MARCIA DONAHUE'S BERKELEY, CALIFORNIA, *garden, a pebble beach complete with colorful bits of sea glass also serves as a pathway. A swinging bench offers a perfect place to escape … and dream.*

BELOW *An open gate is irresistibly welcoming in* SUZANNE PORTER'S BERKELEY, CALIFORNIA, *garden. Choice potted foliage plants include the silvery spears of my favorite plant of the moment,* **Astelia chathamica.** *The plum-colored foliage of* **Loropetalum chinense** *'Razzleberry' and a potted pair of* **Lophomyrtus x ralphii** *'Sundae' reveal that plant sophistication dwells here! All these foliages benefit from the extra shelter they receive by being grown in the often-ignored space between neighboring houses.*

LEFT *Plants will take care of themselves when properly placed. Hydrangeas thrive in the cool, shaded sideyard of* MARK HENRY'S *garden in* SNOHOMISH, WASHINGTON. *A variegated elderberry,* **Sambucus nigra** *'Pulverulenta', adds spectacle and airy variation in height to this mixed planting of shade-loving perennials.*

RIGHT *The already subtle shades of* **Lilium** *'Peach Butterflies' is softened even further when combined with neighboring soft textures. The felted foliage of* **Phlomis fruticosa** *and the wispy grass* **Nassella tenuissima** *combine artfully with* **Hemerocallis** *'Pandora's Box' in the* SEATTLE *garden of the late* STEVE ANTONOW.

RIGHT *Wachendorfia thyrsi-flora's spikes of bright yellow echo the vertical foliage of phormiums and Japanese irises (Iris ensata) in* BOB CLARK'S OAKLAND, CALIFORNIA, *botanical wonderland. A softening tuft of the Japanese grass* **Hakonechloa macra** *'Aureola' clues visitors to choose the left path when given a choice.*

ABOVE *A New Zealand pampas grass,* **Cortaderia richardii,** *arches in a refined focal point in* STEVE ANTONOW'S SEATTLE *garden. It is important to lead the eye, and even more important not to disappoint. David Austin's rose 'Graham Thomas' doubles the beauty quotient without upstaging the star of this vignette.*

RIGHT *"The Elvis Bench" by* RAOUL ZUMBA *provides more than a place to sit in his and* BOB CLARK'S *spectacular* OAKLAND, CALIFORNIA, *garden. Mirror fragments reflect changing falling cherry petals and magnify the beauty all around as disco memories and the seasons go by.*

ONSIDER THE BEAUTY VALUE OF EVERY SURFACE AND DO something about it. A deck doesn't have to remain unadorned. Walls are blank canvases, waiting for a patina of age. I zero in on ancient villa walls in Italy and notice the beautiful staining, left for centuries by wise owners who could well afford to repaint. I have always loved the Italian phrase *bel'occhio*, which roughly translated means "beautiful eye." Plants look much better against a mellowed, knocked-back background.

Make sure your oasis-to-be is not sabotaged by a clinical white paint job. Apartment dwellers and townhouse gardeners may have to disguise rather than repaint. Clever use of trellises, matchstick blinds, bamboo fencing and strategically placed plants can transform a prison cell, let alone a balcony. A bit of "set-dec" is crucial to all forms of gardening.

FACING PAGE ROGER RAICHE *and* DAVID M^cCRORY *have achieved a grotto effect in their* BERKELEY, CALIFORNIA, *garden by planting low-growing* **Acorus gramineus** *'Ogon' in the center of an outstanding collection of foliage. The very beautiful black-stemmed tree fern (**Cyathea medullaris**) is cleverly showcased against an enormous urn. Creating refuges in or of our gardens should be a top priority.*

ABOVE *The entrance court of the* LUNN *garden in* VANCOUVER, B.C., *features a cooling waterfall and unexpected potted tree ferns (**Alsophila australis**). Dramatic foliages spilling from the custom-made bronze containers include the bright purple* **Setcreasea purpurea** *and a burgundy-tinged splash of* **Hakonechloa macra** *'Aureola'. The golden variegated* **Plectranthus** *'Troy's Gold' is only happy in shady situations like this.*

RIGHT *Stone, not plants, provides the landscape in this part of* CEVAN FORRISTT'S SAN JOSE, CALIFORNIA, *garden. This water garden has taken on spiritual importance. Make a wish, or bring an offering? Hmmm …*

ONE OF THE MYSTERIES OF MY LIFE IS REPEATED EVERY DAY. I drive to and from work and cannot help but notice block after block of very average-income homes that appear hopelessly un-gardeny. It is almost a case of one-upmanship to be the most unplanted, least cared for but absolutely occupied. To me, it is a drive through the Valley of Death. Expensive cars, new basketball hoops, satellite television receivers and white plastic patio furniture are everywhere. I ask myself, "What *do* these people care about, anyway?" Occasionally I'll spot a stranded tree peony, blooming its heart out, stoned on ugly. Or a maypole-type clothes-line bedecked with absolutely fried plastic hanging baskets. The botanical equivalent of a car crash.

What I have surmised, with a little help from Joan Rivers, is that "God Divides!" Not everyone received the *bel'occhio* gene. Those of us who did are the lucky ones. We take things like sunsets for granted and get excited over the first snowdrop. We save wrapping paper because it is *so beautiful,* not just to save money and reuse it (well, maybe). Being blessed with what amounts to an extra gene is like having a limitless credit card to go out and treat yourself to a wonderful life. Don't let it expire.

FACING PAGE *A simple copper pipe drips into a pool of lotuses in* CEVAN FORRISTT'S *garden. The sound of water makes us look for its source, and is one way to establish a focal point in even the most interesting of gardens.*

CHAPTER 2 *Dream Big*

REALIZING A SPACE'S POTENTIAL HAS NOTHING TO DO WITH ITS actual size. So those who find themselves gardening in less space shouldn't feel short-changed. Envisioning what could be is actually easier when you're working with physical limitations.

When I garden, I am really setting up for what I hope will be, not what is presently visible. Although my body is working, my mind is months or even years down the road. It has to be. If I stayed in the present, I would never like what I saw. Dreaming while you work is one of gardening's big payoffs. I believe it must create chemical changes in the body. Stress levels disappear, voices become whispers and sore backs don't appear until the next day. The reward is worth any amount of effort.

I have discovered that gardening has no glass ceiling. You will not be held back by anything! The more you read, plant, listen and see, the more you will find available. Instead of going to university, I let the plants teach me. Observing their likes and dislikes gave me a career, a soulmate and a charmed life. Unknowingly, I allowed plants to enslave me as their spokesperson, caretaker and pimp.

PREVIOUS PAGE *The star in this composition of primitive pottery in* DAVIS DOLBAK'S *garden is the chunk of blue slag glass. In cooking, it is the addition of the unexpected that makes one chef better than another.*

FACING PAGE *Why be normal? By adding an architectural fragment of an exotic deity to a stone wall,* CEVAN FORRISTT *has magnified the wall's visual interest many times over. A little déjà vu never hurts.*

Magic — visual and mental —
surrounds DAVIS DOLBAK'S back-
yard swimming pool in SAN
FRANCISCO. A pair of glazed
turquoise jars, a few pieces of
slag glass, and all we see is
turquoise!

RIGHT *On his personal patio, San Francisco retail wizard* DAVIS DOLBAK *has installed a dramatic fire pit amid jungle-like greenery. A substitute for flowers, foliage adds texture and color. The red-tinged* **Ensete ventricosum** *'Maurelii' and the exotic tracery of an Australian tree fern (**Alsophila australis**) create privacy and act as a bold backdrop. Can you imagine white plastic patio chairs in this setting?*

ABOVE *An exotic outdoor living room in* DENNIS SCHRADER *and* BILL SMITH'S LONG ISLAND, NEW YORK, *garden. Tropical foliage, a yellow* **Oncidium** *orchid and a tussle of* **Tillandsia** *on the coffee table suggest faraway places. The Indonesian furniture reinforces the feeling of escape and adventure.*

RIGHT *It's all about texture.* DAVIS DOLBAK'S *grouping of seemingly ancient artifacts share a matte finish and a sense of history. There is time travel in this vignette; a nautical prism catches the light, but who left it there?*

LEFT *Nothing says "come in" (or "stay out") better than a pair of tall gates. A sense of mystery is a very strong lure in* CEVAN FORRISTT'S SAN JOSE, CALIFORNIA, *garden. Plunking an oversize earthenware jar right in the pathway makes its boldness inescapable.*

BELOW *A simple offering or pure decoration, dried zinnias rest beautifully on the feet of a garden statue in* CEVAN FORRISTT'S *garden. Don't forget to say "thank you" every so often.*

I WISH I KNEW WHO SAID, "IT IS NOT IRRITATING TO BE WHERE one is, it is only irritating to wish one was somewhere else." Oscar Wilde? Buddha? Jackie Collins? Regardless, I think this phrase applies perfectly to a lot of people and their gardens. Wishing your garden was better — i.e., less irritating — is a good sign. Now you must allow yourself to dream. Stay with the physical location but change everything else. Using your mind creatively is almost a lost art in the age of digital photos, camera-phones and wireless transmission, but conjuring is unavailable any other way (so far).

"Free your mind, the rest will follow" is a bit of pop radio that shouldn't be forgotten. I use this key phrase when a garden situation has me perplexed. What will look good and grow well together? The answer is not always apparent. Plant labels are not enough, and will not spark any creativity. You've got to let *artistry* do your plant shopping! Artistry is a channel, and you're either tuned in or you aren't. Sometimes you actually see people stumble onto this channel by accident. Watching people shop at a nursery is fascinating — you quickly see who is tuned in!

Dreaming big should be taught in schools. It applies to everything, not just gardening. Stifling potential in people is not only taught, it is sold. Most nurseries sell only common "popular" plants, which immediately limits the gardens in the surrounding neighborhood. Plantaholics will venture further afield, but the majority of homeowners settle for what they can get. I view this as tragic. Who wants to be limited to driving a Chrysler K-Car? I flee from them in traffic, especially if the driver is wearing a white Tilley hat, the dunce cap of the new millennium! The experience is powerful proof that someone forgot to dream.

CHAPTER 3 *The Jewel Box*

Wouldn't it be wonderful if you could describe your garden as a "jewel box full of beautiful plant treasures?" It is entirely possible, and the smaller your outdoor space, the easier it is going to be.

First of all, stop envisioning horizontally. It is much easier to plan from above. Imagine yourself in an art gallery. Instead of staring blankly at one canvas, you are free to float around the room and drink in the entire exhibition. Think of your garden, no matter how small, as an *exhibition space*. This will allow you to see the whole picture as a composite of all your gardening efforts. You still see and enjoy individual details, but rearranging becomes much easier. Is this astral gardening? I hope so.

Once you realize how valuable every square inch is, mediocrity becomes intolerable. Really small-space gardeners can use their eye, but larger-space gardeners will need their feet to make purging rounds, looking for weak spots. There are always plenty, which prompts us to keep tweaking and being creative. It also allows us to keep adding more plants to impossibly full gardens.

PREVIOUS PAGE *Modern hellebores are of such complex breeding they are now referred to as **Helleborus x orientalis** group. The strains keep improving: keep your eyes open for superior flower forms and clear colors. Picoteed petals, double flowers and more upward-facing blooms are waiting for you.*

LEFT *On a tiny balcony in* VANCOUVER, B.C., DAMEN DJOS *creates a fantasy Versailles for himself. True dwarf boxwoods (***Buxus sempervirens** *'Suffruticosa') trained as tiny topiaries, pots of baby's tears (***Soleirolia soleirolii***) and an urn of trailing string of pearls (***Senecio rowleyanus***) all somehow conspire to make the* **Agave americana** *'Variegata' the star.*

BELOW *Tiny spaces are still ruled by scale and proportion. A touch of golden baby's tears (***Soleirolia soleirolii** *'Aurea') softens and marries a miniature cast-iron urn to its terra cotta base on* DAMEN DJOS'S *shady balcony.*

LEFT *A big chunk of cobalt blue glass makes a terrific substitute for flowers for this potted cactus in* ROGER RAICHE *and* DAVID MᶜRORY'S *garden. Unexpected and unexplained, the mysterious deposit is guarded by fierce spines.*

RIGHT ***Pyrus salicifolia*** *'Pendula' still manages to star in this complex planting in* SUSAN RYLEY'S VICTORIA, B.C., *garden. Her trademarked use of mellow yellows and silvery shades receives a well-placed punch from an unnamed dark blue* **Agapanthus** *and the bold spikes of* **Phormium tenax** *foliage.*

RIGHT *A spectacular staging of container plants in* DENNIS SCHRADER *and* BILL SMITH'S LONG ISLAND, NEW YORK, *garden. What appears to be black and white is really lots of green, silver and dark purple.* **Colocasia esculenta** *'Jet Black Wonder' contrasts with the cut-silver foliage of* **Centaurea gymnocarpa**. *The bold white rosettes of a potted pair of* **Furcraea gigantea** *'Striata' guard the entrance to this raised patio area.*

BELOW *At Southlands Nursery in* VANCOUVER, B.C., DAMEN DJOS *created this stunning "chandelier" of* **Rhodochiton atrosanguineum**. *String of pearls (***Senecio rowleyanus***) dangles out the bottom and* **Carex flagellifera** *tosses out the top. Planted and cared for much like a hanging basket, this eye-catching display continued to grow right through our mild winter.*

ABOVE *A collection of jewel-toned foliage softens a step in* SUSAN MACDONALD'S *garden in* SEATTLE. **Coleus, Fuchsia** *'Firecracker',* **Ipomoea batatus** *'Blackie' and the metallic magenta* **Strobilanthes dyerianus** *are now widely available. Sold as bedding plants, all are worth saving indoors over winter in cold climates.*

LEFT *A collection of old garden tools makes a beautiful wall display in* FREELAND TANNER'S CALIFORNIA, *garden. Such displays show personal talent that store-bought decor lacks.*

BELOW *An old bird cage makes an interesting garden accent. I like to change what's in it periodically. This time it houses an octopus-like* **Tillandsia xerographica** *for the summer. My favorite agave,* **Agave americana** *'Mediopicta', gets more appreciation up on a table.*

HAVE YOU NOTICED THAT SMART RETAILERS KNOW THAT WE need a "decompression space" upon entering a store? A bit of space to neutralize, form an instant opinion and be enticed further in. I think they stole this concept from gardening. Whether with a sweeping terrace, a groomed lawn area or an entry court, great gardens begin with some open space, which also keeps the vision changing. Japanese gardens use water this way. An artistic tableau always includes a platform. Those who garden in small spaces need to leave room to breathe, to prevent the Jewel Box from becoming a junk drawer!

The "hardscape" of a garden is often considered less important than the living portion. Good garden designers know that *the two are equals*. This is what separates amateurs from the pros. Patios, pathways, fences and walls should be given first priority, as they contain your dreams. But don't fret — there is a big difference between first and *top* priority, which is reserved for plants. It is for them that you are setting the stage.

Very ordinary surfaces are often inherited with the property, but that doesn't mean you are stuck with them *as is*. Plain concrete patios are the lowest common denominator, and a fact of life for apartment-dwellers. Happily, concrete stains beautifully! What a difference a wash of coppery-green makes. Concrete is also easily scored with a wet saw. Use a chalk snap-line to design a diagonal diamond grid pattern and make shallow cuts in boring concrete to add pattern. It is important to set the stage early in your garden plans. Don't sabotage your garden dreams by ignoring the hardscape.

IT IS TRAGIC THAT MONEY WORRIES CAN STOP PEOPLE FROM achieving anything attractive in their gardens. Lack of funds may excuse you from almost everything else, but it doesn't work this time. So much is free! A collection of stumps can be beautiful, so can rusty barbed wire. "Found objects" and piles of stones blend beautifully with plants. Skeletons of leaves, dried stalks and twigs, old windows and birdcages are all potential scene-stealers *once you realize it*. If necessity is the mother of invention, poverty just might have something to do with creativity. Start looking around and stop coming home empty-handed!

People with limited amounts of outdoor space should consider using plants with extra-value characteristics. Some plants have flashy new spring growth, often tinged in red or peach. The otherwise dreary **Pieris japonica** does this, as does **Euphorbia griffithii.** Herbaceous peonies emerge looking like red licorice, and tree peonies (**Paeonia suffruticosa** hybrids) have new foliage tinged in bronze. This is a very special family of plants that I would never be without. Their floral display in May is so short, it's as if they don't really want us to see it. The message I get from them is, "I'll be gone, so appreciate me now."

Concentrate on plants *that actually give you a thrill* instead of just filling up space or providing "color." For example, I have discovered the modern daylily. Hybridizers have completely transformed the frumpy old **Hemerocallis** into incredible works of art for the garden. They look like the ruffled glass sculptures of Dale Chihuly — imagine an orchid crossed with an Amaryllis that is completely hardy!

Being able to enjoy your Jewel Box from within means creating a place to sit, or even entertain others. The more multifunctional, the better. A barbecue or hot tub has to be attractive as well as functional. Tattoo that on your forehead.

RIGHT *The choice **Aralia elata** 'Aureavariegata' is allowed to star, without competition, in this corner of* TERRY LEBLANC'S VICTORIA, B.C., *garden. Such visually powerful plants need isolation to strut their stuff.*

ABOVE *I employ modern daylilies as secret weapons in my garden. All of a sudden, amazing blooms such as this one — **Hemerocallis** 'Lord of Lightning' — appear from non-descript tufts of green foliage.*

RIGHT ***Hemerocallis** 'Forbidden Desires', one of the finest creations of my daylily guru Ted Petit.*

41

BELOW *Invest in garden lighting! Fixtures must not show. In my own garden, the bark of flowering cherries shows to best advantage at night. A large terra cotta oil jar from Impruneta, Italy, is lit as sculpture. This shady walkway between two houses would be scary if it wasn't nicely lit.*

ABOVE *Search and ye shall find wonder. In the whole world, only* MARCIA DONAHUE *could, and does, have a porch light made from 1960s' swag lamps!*

LEFT *An exotic tapestry planting by* GLENN WITHEY *and* CHARLES PRICE *balances form with color in the* SEATTLE *garden of* BRIAN COLEMAN. *The enormous red leaves of* **Ensete ventricosum** *'Maurelii' are able to compete with the mesmerizing foliage of coleus. Few plants can.*

BRIGHT DAYLIGHT IS THE WORST TIME TO ENJOY YOUR PLANTS or your garden. Colors are bleached out and shadows disappear. Photographers know this. To see what you have achieved, make your rounds earlier or later. After dusk is the most dramatic time of all.

Patterns are exaggerated by adding night lighting. Tiny details can be projected as huge shadows against bare walls. I do this with my wrought-iron gates as well as foliage, projecting squirmy shapes and dramatic, gigantic leaves onto my house at night. I want it to look as weird as possible! For me, *gardening has become theater.* Don't waste space on dull, blobby-shaped plants. I cannot stand heathers or dwarf conifers. The spikes and spears of kniphofias, phormiums, cortaderias and yuccas exude drama. Garden lighting penetrates their open-leaf fountains and travels like neon up to their spiky tips. Roundy-moundy shapes just look like blackened footstools. Leave them for the gas stations.

Creating your own Jewel Box Garden should involve all of your senses. Sight and sound are always there, but taste, touch and scent are optional. Scent adds another dimension to our enjoyment of plants. I get lost there: even fragrance strips in magazines send me. At home, I try to include as many fragrant plants as possible. ***Helichrysum angustifolium***, the curry plant, grows right beside ***Daphne x burkwoodii*** for a wacky olfactory combo. A young ***Daphne bholua*** grows by my front door. I look forward to an immediate hit on winter mornings every time I leave the house. Every year I promise myself I'll grow pots of heliotrope, tubs of tuberoses and bushels of hyacinths (but I haven't yet: so many plants, so little space …). Intoxicating fragrance is something spiritually nutritious and these flowers are giving it away …

FACING PAGE *In my own garden, a Moroccan lantern creates magic! Remember how candles flicker and cast shadows in ways electric lights cannot. Try burning scented candles as well, for an extra scent in the night air.*

CHAPTER 4 *Thinking Like a Plant*

THERE IS MORE TO GARDENING THAN PROVIDING WATER, FERTILIZER and a spot to grow. To get maximum beauty out of your plants, you need to *bond* with them. Like puppies, they are really very easy to please and will show remarkable gratitude for your thoughtful efforts.

Realize that your plants really do depend on you. By thinking like a plant, you will site plants according to *their* wishes, *their* cultural needs, not yours. You will notice signs of stress, such as yellowing leaves, and learn to read them as cries for help, signals to attract your attention. Stop thinking of yourself as a gardener and become an artistic, psychic liaison between plant and animal.

All plants have a common goal — to flower, make seed and ensure their own continuation. To do so, they need help from insects, wind or animals to transfer their pollen. So they make themselves pretty, which happens to appeal to people as well. Realize that they are not putting on this show for *you,* but enjoy it anyway.

One of the last things a dying plant tries to do is flower. This seems very valiant to me, like a sappy movie. The final stages of its life are irreversible. Plants that complete their life cycle in one year are called annuals for a reason, and you must accept this. There is no point whining to hapless nursery employees that your alyssum/stocks/lobelia/marigolds are all done blooming by September, as it is their genetic time clock shutting them down. You can't fight Mother Nature!

PREVIOUS PAGE *Remember "Birds of a feather flock together" when planting. Group plants with the same needs, not the same looks. This allows for creative groupings and healthy plants. These* Echeverias *enjoy each other's company!*

FACING PAGE *The spiral aloe,* Aloe polyphylla, *wants to appear fierce and unmunchable to grazing animals in its native South Africa. Have your face shredded or eat something else — you decide!*

LEFT **Phormium** 'Sundowner' is very happy to see all visitors to the RAICHE/McCRORY *garden in* BERKELEY, CALIFORNIA. *Marcia Donohue's ceramic "additions" help express an already sexy plant's true feelings!*

RIGHT **Hemerocallis** 'Bela Lugosi' *beckons pollinators with its finest offerings. Daylilies really do only have one day to accomplish what most flowers do all summer: get laid! A remarkable, contrasting lime-green throat ensures this daylily will be noticed.*

LEFT *Aeonium arboreum* 'Schwarzkopf' turns darker purple the more sun it gets. Cold-climate gardeners use this plant outside in summer pots and rarely get to see its blinding display of acid-yellow flowers. Other flower colors would disappear in its whorls of darkness.

BELOW *Hemerocallis* 'Sedona', bred by Pat Stamile, is one of my favorite daylilies. It is a perfect color match for my house, but I also love its ruffled gold edge and wide petals. Modern hybridizers have transformed those scraggy, orange things beside the ditch into breathtaking workhorses with names like 'Forbidden Desires' and 'Elusive Dream'.

GREAT-LOOKING, HAPPY PLANTS ARE ALSO HAPPY UNDERGROUND. The part you can't see must be having a good time. To do so, it must have access to air, nutrition and, to varying degrees, moisture. Soil is really a vague term for a whole terrestrial universe. It provides an anchor for plants and a buffet meal they are stuck at for life. Roots will find and absorb nutrients *if they are there.* Soil is dirty hydroponics, using a variety of particles as support for roots as they search for something to eat and drink. This is hard to do without adequate moisture. Ever tried swallowing a pill without a glass of water?

Home gardeners can improve the "meal" in their soil just like organic farmers do. Natural materials such as composted leaves, mushrooms and steer manure add important texture and nutrition to the soil, and encourage an active bacterial component. This makes soil *alive*, which for your plants is like winning the lottery.

It should take years to create a happy soil system. Buying and plunking down "good" soil is not going to help unless it is dug in with what was already there. The earth wants to accept its new layer, but won't do so unless it is married! Many new homeowners find themselves dealing with pancakes of death installed by profit-obsessed contractors. With no attempt to create a *living soil*, plants never really thrive. They are letting you know the cupboard is bare by mysteriously refusing to grow.

BELOW *The icy-blue sprawl of* **Mertensia simplicissima** *and tufts of* **Agropyron magellanicum** *grass create a feeling of dry heat in* LINDA COCHRAN'S *garden on* BAINBRIDGE ISLAND, *near* SEATTLE. *Flat rocks and a faded terra cotta painted wall set a scene far removed from the Pacific Northwest.*

ABOVE *It was the terra cotta wall bracket I wanted, to adorn a plain wall in my garden. Then it made a perfect home for a piece of living sculpture, a very kooky* **Cryptocereus** *I paired with a small sculpted tile by Bay area artist Mark Bullwinkle.*

LEFT *You know this* **Agave parryi** *wants sun, just by its appearance. Silvery colors and spines are clues, but its wide-open leaf arrangement is really a solar panel designed to catch as much light as possible and create little shadow. Notice the subtle tattoos created by the sun as leaves unfurl, one on top of another.*

THIS SIGN OF UNHAPPINESS WILL LAST FOREVER UNLESS YOU take action. You need to improve the soil down where the plants are grazing. Stopping plant suicide is nearly impossible. It can be done, but it takes a long time to nurse a sentimental favorite back to health. A spa treatment, severe amputation or shock treatments may be necessary. I have tried massive doses of fertilizer, but soon learned that it was the weakest plants that overdosed. Plants on their last legs seem most willing to offer a cutting, a small part of themselves as a legacy of hope for the future. Withered orchids, dessicated jade plants and tortured pelargoniums can often be rescued and regrown from last-gasp tips.

Thinking like a plant means putting yourself in the plant's place for a while. How would you like to sit in front of your hot air duct in the living room all winter? Envision those *Ficus benjamina* leaves as skin flakes falling off. Then you die.

Television commercials have finally taught us about SP factor and tanning. Sun protection is now common sense, except when it comes to placing newly bought, greenhouse-grown plants outside. Many leaves are permanently scalded by this transfer to reality. Avoid this by first resting them under a shade tree for a day or two. Give the plants time to adjust their leaf surfaces after the cushy world of the greenhouse.

Make yourself more aware of how similar we are to plants. You should thrill them as much as they thrill you. The best gardeners have balanced relationships going with their gardens. A happy marriage. Any reward is incidental, but not unnoticed. In good times and bad … sickness and health … I do.

FACING PAGE *Cascading or trailing plants need to be displayed to best advantage. This means off the ground. I grow the hybrid oregano* **Origanum** *'Barbara Tingey' in an Italian terra cotta pot atop a garden wall, where its waterfall of ornamental "hops" delights me — and countless bees — all summer long.*

LEFT *If you've got it, flaunt it.* **Cornus controversa** *'Variegata' must always be treated like a star. In* SUSAN RYLEY'S VICTORIA, B.C., *garden, it reigns supreme in the back corner of what is really a bank vault, not a jewel box of a garden.*

RIGHT *String of pearls (***Senecio rowleyanus***) adds a fabulous fringe to* DAMEN DJOS'S *potted agave on his* VANCOUVER, B.C., *balcony.*

CHAPTER 5 *It's All About Me*

T HE PLANTS YOU CHOOSE TO "PLAY WITH" END UP SAYING A LOT
about you. "Saying it with flowers" is a valid form of
expression. Try to adopt this slogan as your gardening
mantra. Keep it in mind while plant shopping as well as when
actually planting. How much are you willing to reveal?

Really good gardeners don't hold back. Mesmerizing, memorable
plant pictures are created by the brave. Spines, teeth, spikes, thorns
and even seed capsules add an edginess to plant compositions.
"Safe" gardeners rely on flowers alone and leave theatricality out of
it. Gardening is a chance to spread your wings — why do so many
people never fly?

Beware of the botanical quicksand sold as "annuals." This
huge industry dispenses humdrum goop like "supertunias" and
the insanely popular bacopa (**Suteria cordata**). This trailing, white-
flowered annual is the botanical equivalent of icicle lights — so
overused and trite it has lost any attractiveness through overex-
posure. The discerning eye learns to avoid most popular plants.
Why be like everyone else?

PREVIOUS PAGE *Cerinthe major* '*Purpurescens*' *froths about like a neon purple
eucalyptus, while succulent* **Echeverias** *and the very dark purple* **Sedum x**
'*Bertrum Anderson*' *bake in the sun in my small patio pocket garden.* **Phormium**
'*Sundowner*' *adds another foliage texture to an already busy mixture.*

LEFT *In a small, shady corner of my garden, baby's tears (**Soleirolia soleirolii**) carpet the moist soil. A collection of old wooden fence finials forms a sculptural grouping in a "foliage only" composition. The silver-splashed, evergreen leaves of **Asarum splendens** are allowed to star, while the bizarre "tatting fern," **Athyrium filix-femina** 'Frizelliae', looks on. A self-sown **Alchemilla mollis** and **Hosta** 'Gold Standard' frame this tableau of less than one square yard.*

BELOW *The incredibly beautiful **Saxifraga fortunei** 'Miyuki's Purple' at Heronswood Nursery in Kingston, Washington.*

As you spend more time gardening, you develop a need for higher highs, a botanical fix that never satisfies. Walking around a nursery becomes more of a mission than an excursion. Avid gardeners become plant sharks, circling plant sales, hoping to score. This is what happens as you become a plant *addict*. Some become obsessed collectors who stash their hoard artlessly. Thankfully, most are changed into superb, artistic gardeners. They join a universal plant community whose members recognize each other instantly. Mutual respect is granted or withheld in direct proportion to botanical knowledge. Plant savvy has often led to friendship, even marriage. The mutual love of plants has an instant bonding effect, even amongst strangers.

Certain plants are practically an entree in themselves. Hellebores worked for several years, but are now losing their power; there are too many around. Double-flowered hellebores (the **Helleborus x orientalis** group) still enchant me, as do green-flowered species such as **Helleborus viridis**. The very dark-flowered, near-black hybrids are still in my garden, but no longer in my heart. It took five or six years, but the thrill of their funereal spring show is gone. A double-flowered black one is the hit I need now!

FACING PAGE *An antique plant stand from France holds personal favorites up where I can appreciate them. Pots of **Saxifraga fortunei** (the brown cultivar 'Velvet' and the multi-hued 'Five Color') would get lost in the garden. **Arthropodium candidum** is just the right brownish color to complement this grouping. This New Zealand native appears grass-like but is actually in the lily family.*

ABOVE *The first time I saw* **Podophyllum delavayi**, *I screamed. This spectacular "Mayapple" from China is my most prized plant. I have grown it in a pot for years, and will now plant it out in moist, dappled shade.*

RIGHT *The hardy cyclamen are true jewels for almost anyone's garden. Patiently grown from seed, many spectacular forms are to be seen at Heronswood Nursery. This spectacular clump is from* **Cyclamen hederifolium** *'Bowle's Apollo group' seed. Needless to say, I am now growing some tiny seedlings myself.*

THERE IS SOMETHING EXTRA CHARMING ABOUT "SHY" PLANTS. I will stop what I am doing to admire the nodding flowers of **Deinanthe caerulea**. This herbaceous hydrangea relative from China produces clusters of nodding, waxy flowers in mid-summer. With particularly refined, cupped petals arranged very formally around a central "button," individual flowers appear as fine porcelain treasures.

I am also enchanted with the charm of many **Ranunculus ficaria** cultivars. These early bloomers, which come in bronzy-foliaged forms like 'Brazen Hussy' and 'Brambling', fill cracks between my steps. The small bright-gold flowers look like tiny calendulas atop miniature water lily foliage. Their show is completely over by late May, forcing me to really admire them while I can. One of my most treasured small perennials is the variegated **Hacquetia epipactis** 'Thor'. This subtle charmer produces celadon green- and white-striped flowers and foliage! Most people walk right past its discreet beauty. But I bought my car because it was the same shade of green as 'Thor'!

Being a left-handed, Gemini breach-birth *allows* me to love tetraploid daylilies. It is *who I am botanically*. Being able to appreciate the smaller, charming plants as well as the bold and dramatic makes me feel well rounded as a gardener. It also makes me believe in astrology. I am such a Gemini!

FACING PAGE *Deinanthe caerulea is a seldom-encountered, herbaceous relative of the hydrangea. I am smitten with its porcelain-like, soft lavender flowers*

LEFT *'Ed Brown' is one of the most beautiful of all* **Hemerocallis**. *In my garden, he co-opts the gorgeous foliage of a neighboring* **Symphytum uplandicum** *'Variegatum' rather than admit to his own.*

BELOW *Moist cracks in my front stairs hold treasures. The lilac–blue* **Anemone nemerosa** *'Allenii' shares tight quarters with various color forms of* **Ranunculus ficaria**. *These spring ephemerals ask for nothing, and are dormant by June.*

HOW YOU COMPOSE YOUR PLANTS IS THE HARD PART. THERE are shelves full of books on this subject and this is another one. Combining plants artistically is easier if you know a few basic rules regarding harmony, proportion and contrast. Combining these with good "plant requirement" (basic care) knowledge results in interesting and healthy planting.

Whether in containers or the open garden, plants always group best in triangular blocks. The eye can only drink in so much at a time, so it is best to have a "leader" — a high shape the eye is drawn to — supported by lower, blobbier underplantings on either side or in front. I compose most pots by planting a taller plant at the back first, then working forward, building a slope effect toward the front.

In a mixed planting, never put the tallest plant in the center of the pot. Doing that immediately gives one away as artless. If a pot is to be seen from all sides, plant three tall things in the middle instead of one. They don't all have to be the same, either. Try combining a young New Zealand flax (a **Phormium** cultivar of your choice), a bronze **Carex flagellifera** and a dark-leaved dahlia such as 'Bednall Beauty' or 'Ellen Houston'. This is much more visually interesting than a green dracaena 'spike' (**Cordyline australis**), the last refuge of the truly desperate.

THE SHAPE OF THE ACTUAL CONTAINER SHOULD DICTATE THE end result. Low, wide pots are the most attractive, offering more "tabletop" space to plant in. Pots that are wider than they are tall look more anchored and group themselves more easily. There is nothing wrong with the typical, cone-shaped flowerpot, but why be typical? Limit yourself to one taller pot per grouping, flanked by a cluster of two or more non-identical, lower pots. This is the way to create "eye candy."

When grouping plant containers, don't mix too many textures or materials in close proximity. Stick to one overall theme per cluster: either plain terra cotta, glazed, metallic or wood. Plastic is not an option. Seriously! The plants themselves should overpower every container visually — if they don't, you'd better start over. I remember feeling sorry for the cherub-bedecked, bronze urns at Versailles. Each contained one scraggly pelargonium, dying of an inferiority complex and pleading, "Please take me" to every tourist.

Cerinthe major 'Purpurescens', succulent **Echeverias**, dark purple **Sedum x** 'Bertrum Anderson' and **Phormium** 'Sundowner' on my patio garden. Notice the white tags on my daylily? I am hybridizing them now, instead of orchids!

CHAPTER 6 *Benefits Package*

I LIKE TO ASK A PLANT, "WHAT HAVE YOU DONE FOR ME LATELY?" Color, scent and even sound should figure in the reply. I am a sucker for color and am ready to hop into bed (the garden bed, these days) with anything silver, celadon green or violet purple. I also require massive doses of rust, apricot and chartreuse. Interestingly, these colors all look good together in virtually any combination. Celadon green and silver are neutral. Purple is a standout, the alpha wolf of the garden. It dominates but allows rusty and apricot shades to play second fiddle.

Review your own color preference and allow a natural order to occur. If you thrive on red and yellow combinations, you are reading the wrong book. Red and orange is exciting, orange and yellow is tolerable but limited, but red and yellow is artless and screams "Gas Station." There are too many other beautiful combinations out there to ever plant red and yellow together. The glaucous-blue, trailing foliage of *Mertensia simplicissima* (absolute slug caviar) with acid-green *Carex elata* 'Bowle's Golden' grass nearby is pure eye candy. I love blue with green, and rely on this combo as an understudy in my own garden. Hosta 'June' is well behaved and provides a hit of blue with green, as does *Nicotiana langsdorfii* with its amazing robin's-egg-blue pollen and apple-green flowers.

PREVIOUS PAGE *It is important to grow* **Mertensia simplicissima** *out of reach of slugs and snails, which will quickly destroy its beautiful blue foliage. I was surprised to find how happy it is in containers.* **Carex elata** *'Bowle's Golden' makes a screamingly good neighbor for just about anything! Using perennials in pots is not illegal, you know.*

FACING PAGE **Dicentra** *'Snowflakes' is a perfect color match for slate steps in my garden. Its glaucous-blue foliage takes on a natural tan by midsummer and complements my peachy walls. A polite spreader with crisp white flowers in spring, this hardy perennial is faultless.*

LEFT *Autumn color is a benefit to seek out. The* **Hamamelis** *or witch hazel family includes virtual superstars of autumn glory, such as the coppery-flowered variety 'Jelena', which has superb fall color. Witch hazels become small trees and are perfectly suited for city gardens. Their upright, vase-shaped growth habit allows you to plant woodland treasures underneath.*

BELOW *The pleated leaves of* **Veratrum nigrum** *are beautiful works of nature's art. Reminiscent of origami, they are really designed to funnel and shed rainwater.*

Y OU WON'T ACHIEVE THAT "MAGAZINE LOOK" IN YOUR GARDEN until you get the color combinations right. "I'm ready for my close-up" should always be kept in mind when placing a new plant. I assemble plant montages quite slowly. I may find the perfect plant partners two or three years apart. Shifting and regrouping is what gardening becomes; the endless pursuit of perfection. It is hardly drudgery! Playing with plants is safest in spring or fall, but container-grown perennials and shrubs are often irresistible in summer. They don't really feel the move if watered and cared for.

Gardening with limited space should force a high content of "double-duty" plants. Fragrance becomes more important at close range and can instantly alter your mood. Try, if at all possible, to grow a daphne. Daphnes range in hardiness, and almost all are divinely scented. I am particularly fond of **Daphne odora**, whose early spring fragrance carries spicy notes of clove and carnation unusual distances. This broadleaf, evergreen shrub forms a wide, low mound and is happiest when *not* in a pot.

Everyone should grow heliotropes. This favorite of the Victorian era possesses a particularly mood-altering fragrance that immediately cheers people up. It is foolproof as a summer annual and comes in shades of white, mauve or dark purple. I time-travel back to my childhood barbershop every time I smell heliotrope, because the barber used to dust my neck with talcum powder when he was done. Fragrance and memory seem to share shelf space in the brain. Several times I have felt the need to ask total strangers, "What *is* that perfume you're wearing?" Every time it has turned out to be Shalimar by Guerlain. I wish I could grow something even remotely as incredible; the scent immobilizes me.

FACING PAGE *We are all slaves to fragrance, and there is a scent for everyone. Thankfully, lavender has lost its "granny" stigma and is now welcome in even the hippest gardens. Try some in ice cream or crème brûlée!*

ANOTHER FEATURE TO LOOK OUT FOR IS UNUSUAL LEAF TEXTURE. Not just smooth or fuzzy, but unique qualities like accordion pleating or the way water reacts to the leaf surface. I grow the tropical, palm-like grass **Setaria palmifolia** for its pleated blades, which are very sculptural in themselves. The hardy **Veratrums** also have fabulous folded leaves that clasp the stem; they bring the fashions of Japanese designer Issey Miyake to mind.

I am still amazed when watching water droplets bead up and bounce off the leaves of the elephant's ear plant (**Colocasia**). The black-leaved form, **Colocasia esculenta** 'Black Magic', is especially worth owning. By some kind of evolutionary magic, water becomes mercury-like and rolls off these plants, leaving absolutely no trace of wetness. It's a botanical parlor trick and nature's own Scotchgard!

Sometimes it is necessary to bruise or crush a plant to (hopefully) enjoy its added dimension. The various types of lavender (**Lavendula** species) have never been as popular as they are today. Only a few years ago they were regarded as "granny plants," but no more. Inhaling fresh or dried lavender is immediately beneficial and affects everyone. It also makes fantastic flavoring in plain ice cream! Many people like the peanut-butter scent of bruised **Melianthus major** foliage. I can't stand this scent, but love the saw-toothed, nearly blue foliage of this tender South African native. Another plant I grow but avoid bruising is the bulbous **Nectaroscordum siculum**. This **Allium** relative gets to stay in my garden because of the rigid stems of sophisticated, molasses-striped, beige bells it produces in springtime. If I accidentally break or bruise a bud or leaf when digging nearby, I soon regret it as the gassy odor makes me gag.

FACING PAGE *Watch as leaves change color. This show is free and is often taken for granted. Plants cope with sun just as people do, by adjusting their skin. This aloe is putting on a fine show in midsummer. During periods of less sun, its leaves turn significantly greener.*

In the TORONTO *garden of* NANCY AND TOM LAURIE, *a spectacular series of jets forms a stunning backdrop to a formal urn focal point. Such "water tricks" were popular centuries ago in aristocratic European gardens and were often turned on just as guests passed by. I would love to operate one of these by remote control, especially if it shot sideways!*

BELOW *Beautifully tiled in slate mosaic, a small wall niche water feature by my front door holds a few glass fishing floats. Serving no purpose other than visual delight, they move about in an imaginary game of snooker.* **Fuchsia magellanica** *'Molinae' dangles above.*

ABOVE *Unnaturally exciting color is created by kooky background screens in this magic moment by California's* CEVAN FORRISTT. *The brilliant green bamboo stalks are matched in clarity of color by the interior glaze of an intentionally empty Asian pottery bowl. The three elements contribute equally in a perfectly edited vision.*

84

YOU MAY FIND CERTAIN PLANTS ATTRACT WELCOME VISITORS. Hummingbirds are attracted to tubular-shaped flowers, especially reddish ones. They love **Phygelius**, the Cape fuchsia, and will visit nectar-rich **Cannas**. Many people try to attract butterflies by planting a "butterfly garden," which sounds delightful. In reality, these seeds-in-a-can mixtures result in a weed patch of dull "wildflowers" that only lasts one season. I think butterflies hate people and are better left on their own.

Sound, on a small scale, is very personal. Most plants remain silent their entire lives, though large trees get to rustle in the wind, especially in autumn. We can add limited amounts of sound to our gardens, but it's risky. Wind chimes are dreadful intrusions into neighborhoods: just because you like them doesn't mean the people next door do. I think they are as bannable as leaf blowers.

Water features can bring a pleasantness to a garden, providing a variety of benefits. Large jets cool the air, mask street noise and are always attractive. The simpler, the better. A plain, skyward jet of water should emerge from the simplest possible basin. Homeowners can scale down to suit their space. Even a balcony can feature a small fountain of some type. Pleasant sounds help us escape and *make* us relax, no stereo required. Realizing that creating an outdoor space involves more than just plants is what brings it all together. Don't just fill your needs, include your *desires*.

"My master is the tree outside my window"

ANTONIO GAUDÍ

FACING PAGE *A massive Garry oak,* **Quercus garryana**, *waits outside* TERRY LE BLANC'S VICTORIA, B.C., *kitchen doors. The beauty of its bark and sheer presence is humbling. Our obsession with foliage and flowers seems so shallow when you see a magnificent plant like this.*

CHAPTER 7 *Boogie Oogie Oogie*

CERTAIN COMBINATIONS ARE HARD TO FORGET. I AM STILL reeling from seeing Kristy McNichol and former TV talk show host Mike Douglas singing "Get Down, Boogie Oogie Oogie" together. They were wearing matching red overalls and descending a blinking, backlit Plexiglas staircase. Twenty-five years later, the damage is still unhealed in my brain. Gardeners have to be careful, too. What was once considered trendy and bold might actually be really ugly.

I feel partially responsible for the recent "zonal denial" craze. Many gardeners found a new kind of liberation by planting just about anything, anywhere. The results were rarely good. Mixing "exotics" with each other is fairly safe, but adding a random bit of "tropicalissimo" into average planting only looks like botanical vandalism. Foliar graffiti.

Creating a *cohesive* plant picture should be your goal. Imagine you are casting a play and each plant is a possible cast member. Will everyone get along? You will need to eliminate plant personality clashes. Dry-growing plants do fine together. Shade lovers unite, and sun-worshippers are happy en masse. Then, looking deeper into each group, you can start to really fine-tune the picture. Noticing foliage's own merit has to come first; flowers, if any, are a bonus. Being able to combine foliage is what earns you respect from other gardeners. This is gardening's highest level of achievement.

PREVIOUS PAGE *Coleus* 'Tilt a Whirl' *reignited my love affair with this genus of plant playthings. Its exciting leaf shape suggests movement as well as exhibiting gorgeous colors. Multihued leaves offer greater possibilities for playing around when choosing what to plant next to what.*

LEFT *Dahlia 'Ellen Houston' is a Canadian-bred variety beloved worldwide. Coppery-black foliage is the perfect foil to its burnt-orange flowers. Limited-space gardeners need to make use of "double value" plants like this one whenever possible: great foliage and great flowers are not common.*

BELOW *Instead of a clash,* **STEVE ANTONOW** *has achieved a symphony effect with the same* **Pleioblastus auricomus** *bamboo. The acid-green color is amplified by* **Hosta** *'Gold Standard' and a clump of* **Hakonechloa macra** *'Aureola' grass. Even the dreaded, invasive Bishop's Weed (**Aegopodium podagraria** 'Variegatum') looks good, this time!*

RIGHT *Dahlia 'Bednall Beauty' is showcased against* **Pleioblastus auricomus** *(syn.* **P. viridistriatus***) in* **STEVE ANTONOW'S SEATTLE** *garden. His expert contrast of two very striking foliages allows for better appreciation of each. A touch of silvery* **Plectranthus argentatus** *in the foreground acts as a neutralizer in this pleasant clash.*

A complete contrast in every respect, the dazzle of **Gingko biloba**'s *autumn farewell is sliced by blades of dark canna foliage in* NANCY HECKLER's *garden near* SEATTLE. *It is an amazing but fleeting lesson in color combination from Mother Nature herself.*

ABOVE *The shuttlecock-like flowers of an* **Abutilon** *pick out the squash-yellow shades in an otherwise peachy* **Phormium** *in* MARCIA DONAHUE's *garden in* BERKELEY, CALIFORNIA.

RIGHT *I like to use coleus to reinforce more subtle neighbors in my own plantings. The peachy stripes of* **Phormium** *'Sundowner' absorb some red from* **Coleus** *'Coral Glo' and look even better.*

RIGHT **Corydalis flexuosa** 'Purple Leaf' brings a unique hue of flower and foliage to shady garden areas. I like it the best of all the **Corydalis**, as it is vigorous but not invasive. Smoky purple is a color seldom found in flowers. Just a bit mysterious, it combines beautifully with the acid-green creeping foliage of **Lysimachia nummularia** 'Aurea' and the green-flowered primrose 'Francisca' in my own garden.

BELOW 'Bright Lights' is a seed strain of Swiss chard that makes an unforgettable winter ornamental in the Pacific Northwest. Its neon leafstalks thrive in and illuminate the weeks of drizzly rain. Gardeners elsewhere should grow it as a tropical imposter until really hot weather makes it go to seed.

ABOVE **Hosta** 'Sagae' is a big beauty. In moist soil and light shade it forms an imposing and almost slug-proof clump worth every inch of the space it needs! I remove its occasional flower stalks as they only detract from the vision of perfect foliage.

RELYING ON FOLIAGE WOULD BE NO FUN IF ALL WE HAD TO WORK with was the color green. I would only last twenty seconds. We can literally thank God for the multitude of silvers, golds, biscuit browns, purples, reds, celadon greens and mesmerizing variegations he gave us to play with.

Foliage effects last much longer than flowers and are always more subtle. Leaves emerge one shade, expand to another and finally die, often in a spectacular farewell. Often (as with hostas), any blossoms are detrimental. Exceptions are deliberately placed beauties (such as lilies) that appear, do their thing, then go away.

Successful plant pictures will either happen instantly or take *way too long*. Sometimes the "missing link" shows up months later and what was okay becomes *exceptional*. This happens to me every year! Either I can't find a certain shade of **Diascia** or someone has introduced an amazing new **Coleus**. I will attack and redo at any time if something more exciting catches my eye. The missing link!

FACING PAGE *What a difference a plant makes!* **Coleus** *'Coral Glo' steals the scene every time.* **Fuchsia** *'Gartenmeister Bohnstedt' and* **F.** *'Baby Chang' are deliberate color choice "echoes" in my shady border. Keeping the soil very moist produces lush growth.*

LEFT *A lesson in foliage shapes and color combination in* STEVE ANTONOW'S *garden. Golden fingers of* **Hakonechloa macra** *'Aureola' match* **Hosta** *'Gold Standard' in color but not in shape, texture or habit. The neutral blue foliage of* **Hosta** *'Halcyon' helps tone down the wattage.*

RIGHT **Brunnera** *'Jack Frost' is one of the best hardy new perennials. Its silvery foliage looks tropical, but isn't. Summertime sprays of no-big-deal blue flowers are best removed, to maintain a bold effect. Play up the silvery blue by choosing plants such as* **Festuca** *'Golden Toupee' for neighbors.*

RIGHT *Kalanchoe thyrsiflora* is a scene-stealer. Its cartoon-like paddles redden in the sun and are somehow amusing. Deliberately underplanted with less interesting **Sedum** and **Echeveria**, it is displayed to maximum advantage in a shallow clay pot.

ABOVE **Colocasia antiquorum** 'Illustris' is an exotic but easy-to-grow taro with black-suffused leaves. It loves summer heat and shallow water. Grow it in a shiny, glazed black container to amplify its unique feature.

RIGHT **Pelargoniums** (sold, incorrectly, as geraniums) can have incredible foliage. Complex ring patterns can be cleverly "separated" using matching but solid-colored neighboring plants.

TRAIN YOURSELF TO LOOK CLOSELY, AND NOTICE THAT ALL foliage contains patterns. Many are spectacular, so you have to watch what you mix together. Just like getting dressed, there are rules even I don't break. Don't mix checks and spots. Variegation is best in smallish doses. There is a big difference between burberry and the Bay City Rollers!

Spectacular, eye-popping color can really only "pop" if you allow it to. Determine which plant is destined to be "Number One" and build your hit parade around it. Variegated plants hate playing second fiddle. Only a characteristic such as near-black foliage has more power than they do.

Some gardeners will never learn the art of plant assemblage. Try how they might, they are oblivious to what is missing. Things appear healthy and happy, *but dull*. These are the people who keep nurseries in business, their trunks filled with impulse purchases and flats of annuals. As I drive by their predictable efforts, I often wonder, "Is life easier?"

FACING PAGE *Subtlety has its place. Irish moss (**Sagina sublata** 'Aurea') forms an undulating ground cover, but dislikes foot traffic. Not a true moss, it is reminiscent of woodland glades and perfect for a Zen moment in the Jewel Box Garden.*

CHAPTER 8 *Gilding the Lily*

INTRODUCING NONLIVING ELEMENTS INTO YOUR OUTDOOR SPACE is what makes it memorable. Sometimes they can also make it laughable, so you have to be careful. There is an entire industry devoted to tomorrow's landfill: garden décor.

Although I enjoy placing beautiful objects in strategic spots in my garden, I have never deliberately gone out and bought anything to fill that role. It just seems to happen. Adding nonliving elements to the garden is the icing on the cake: it should be done last. Wait until plants have grown in and let them suggest where you have a void. This way, you avoid the "garden makeover" look, where everything is instant and phony looking. Your involvement with any item of garden decoration has to be personal.

I am reluctant to use the phrase "focal point," as it has lost its meaning. Too many homeowners have gone out shopping for one. How about a wishing well or a concrete seal pup with a ball on its nose? Who wants only one?

Any time your eye stops and focuses, you've got a *focus point*, like it or not. It might be a dead rat, or a mildewed rosebush could be stealing the scene in its own hateful way. What is lacking in many otherwise successful planted areas is what I refer to as an "item." This is all-encompassing and neutral enough to mean almost anything except a plant. An "item" is something covetous and slightly valuable. It is code. It means something good.

PREVIOUS PAGE *The refined quietness of green-on-green creates an appropriate setting for a classical statue in* MARK HENRY's *garden. The sculptural shapes of nearby plants are kept simple, to keep our attention focused on the statue.*

MARK HENRY's *dreams of Venice, Italy, flutter in his* SNOHOMISH, WASHINGTON, *garden. Well-tended clusters of pots help marry the house to the garden, and colors are expertly extracted from the flag above.*

*A very beautiful Italian terra cotta figure holds a basket of string of pearls (**Senecio rowleyanus**) on her head at* SOUTHLANDS NURSERY *in* VANCOUVER, B.C. *Happy in little soil and a perfect match in feeling, this plant is what sold the statue.*

BELOW *This lead mask from England looks down and over my hot tub, as a reminder not to stay in too long!*

ABOVE *A glazed figure of a blackamoor from Florence, Italy, waits by my front door.* **Agave americana** *'Mediopicta' is beautiful enough to compete, but just barely. Both come inside for the winter.*

BELOW *Purple paint power!* DANIEL SPARLER *and* JEFF SCHOUTEN'S *use of bold color goes beyond plants in their* SEATTLE, WASHINGTON *garden. Massive doses of in-your-face paint turn what was already eye candy into mind candy!*

ABOVE *A bowl of ceramic fruit in the* RAICHE/MᶜCRORY GARDEN *is made even more interesting by tucking in a few undemanding* **Echeveria**. *What is real and what is not is a mind game that should exclude anything plastic.*

LEFT *A bright purple umbrella from Bali zaps up the scene in another part of* MARK HENRY'S *garden. The magenta blossoms of* **Geranium maderense** *and the gunmetal mauve foliage of* **Rosa glauca** *both seem to draw bonus color from this perky prop.*

LEFT *Potted bowling balls are hard to kill.* MARCIA DONAHUE *welcomes visitors to her* BERKELEY, CALIFORNIA, *home with a row she grew from seed.*

BELOW **Sempervivums** *surround weird little Tiki gods in* BOB CLARK *and* RAOUL ZUMBA'S GARDEN. *A sense of humour makes visiting a garden much more fun.*

TARTING UP THE GARDEN WITH TOO MANY YUM-YUMS IS A PITFALL not just reserved for the rich. Although I have winced at more plastic in gardens than anything else, bronze has recently become mentally toxic to me. How can I delete visions of cast-bronze children chasing a frog, or Grandma welded to a park bench?

Mass-produced items also lack appeal. Concrete *anything,* unless dripping with plants, is too ordinary. There is something less desirable about products when you know a factory is shipping them everywhere. It keeps them out of my garden: I would rather buy something out of town and have it shipped home, to remind me of my holiday. Garden ornaments, "items," have to be, in some way, works of art. They don't have to be museum quality, but they have to involve emotional *thought.* It should be *you* floating glass fishing floats in a pool of water, deliberately staging something beautiful. Make your own birdbath instead of buying one.

Placing your treasures should be a gut reaction. Obvious homes for "items" are on walls, steps and nestled amongst plants. My rule is that I should only be able to see one non-plant treasure per glance. Keep things apart, so you will appreciate their beauty and the contribution they make to your personal oasis. The less space you have, the more you have to really treasure your garden accessories. Only use the meaningful.

We all admire antique garden statuary in European gardens. It is *appropriate to time and place.* Remember that, and apply it to your own space. Bowling balls are appropriate in Marcia Donahue's garden/gallery in Berkeley, California, because *she did it first.* It's a wacky place, and if your garden isn't, no bowling balls for you!

LEFT *Although there are many beautiful bamboos in nature, none are quite as colorful as Marcia's own ceramic creations. This potted fantasy is too good to be true; part plant, part sculpture and no care required.*

RIGHT *I realized my home's blank stucco walls were potential canvases, waiting for dabs of ornament. This cast stone cherub keeps aging and improving in appearance. My very own Portrait of Dorian Gray?*

RIGHT A *"mulch" of rocks is so much more interesting than bark chips would have been in* NANCY *and* TOM LAURIE'S TORONTO *garden. The smooth trunk of a dwarf Japanese maple* (Acer palmatum *cultivar) benefits visually by association.*

ABOVE *Remember, surfaces are often underfoot, but not invisible. In* JOHN RAMSAY'S VANCOUVER, B.C., *townhouse garden, designer John Minty created a patterned surface. Dark, smooth pebbles fill deliberate voids in a recycled concrete-paver terrace.*

RIGHT *Granite cobblestones in* NANCY KENNEDY'S TORONTO *garden set a formal rhythm in motion. Clipped balls of ever-green* Euonymus *and collars of English ivy create a sophisticated sculpture court.*

CHAPTER 9 *Casa Triangulo*

Nestled on a steep hill high above a beach known as Spanish Banks sits one of Vancouver's best examples of an architectural style known as Mission Revival. Built in 1933, the house was the home of Dr. Joseph Kania, who was also its architect. He moved to British Columbia from Los Angeles during the Depression, when the only job he could find was "up here" at a securities firm. He decided to recreate an L.A. dream home in Vancouver.

I first saw "Kania Castle," as it was known in the neighborhood, in 1975. A friend drove me by in his sports car, knowing I would be enchanted by its faded Hollywood awnings and intricate tile roof. I was more than enchanted: I nearly got whiplash. The house was surrounded by huge trees, many of which had been "topped" to improve neighbors' views. The street was still unpaved at that time and hard to find, and the house looked almost abandoned. Strings of old Christmas lights were falling off the eaves and a stuffed pheasant stared out of the living room window. On the cliff side, concrete stairs with rickety wooden handrails rose through blackberries. I returned occasionally to sneak around. There were three underground garages! I imagined Norma Desmond's car was still in one of them; "Max" was probably watching me from the living room.

PREVIOUS AND FACING PAGE *Giant* **Chamaecyparis lawsoniana** *trees dwarf my house in Vancouver, B.C. Many similar ones are dying of a deadly phytopthera organism in the groundwater. I hope my steep hillside's excellent drainage saves them.* **Trachycarpus fortunei** *palms,* **Euphorbia characias** *'Wulfenii' and the white spikes of* **Yucca recurvifolia** *enhance the Spanish architecture.* **Magnolia** *'Forrest's Pink' appears as a green blob, but in spring is a complete knockout with its bubble-gum-pink blizzard of 10-inch blossoms.*

LEFT *My front walkway is planted with muddy colors and includes favorite daylilies. The gold-edged purple 'Scott Fox' and peachy 'Pizza Crust' bloom with bronze* **Carex flagellifera** *and bluish* **Echeverias**.

BELOW *Along my front walk, the dried orb of* **Allium schubertii** *appears to have landed from another galaxy. The self-sown purple bells of* **Cerinthe major** *'Purpurascens' are always welcome, but dry up by late July.* **Hemerocallis** *'Scott Fox' and an unusual white-flowered* **Calceolaria alba** *from Chile welcome me home.*

I BECAME OBSESSED WITH THE HOUSE AND BEGAN STALKING IT. I was terrified someone would buy it and tear it down. It had spectacular views of downtown, the mountains and the harbor. I returned many times to make sure it was still there. The pheasant in the window never moved. I could tell "old" people lived there. *Nothing* ever changed.

By this time my young flower shop was getting on its feet. I had no money, but every top real estate agent was using me to send flowers to their best clients. I gave one of them the address and asked her to find out what she could about the house. She did, and I felt hopeless. It was way out of my wildest dreams dollar-wise. I kept the piece of paper anyway. I remember staring at it, thinking how odd it would be to garden on a triangular lot, living in a triangular house …

Several snoopy visits later I decided to write a letter to the house. It was 1977, and I was 23 years old. I said I was in love with the house and hoped, one day, to be able to afford it. I also said that I was worried that someone else might tear it down. I would never do that. I would restore it and protect it.

Ten years later my florist shop phone rang. A little old man introduced himself as Joe Kania, and asked me point blank if I still wanted to buy his house. I said, "the *Spanish* one?"

LEFT *We built this sweeping terrace to maximize our views of downtown Vancouver. A planting pocket holds an ever-taller* **Trachycarpus fortunei** *palm. Uplit at night, it is easy to imagine oneself on the Riviera. I soon stopped wrapping my palms for the winter as they have proven to be totally hardy. Gold-leaved* **Fuchsia** *'Genii',* **Ballotta pseudodictamnus** *and* **Abutilon** *'Melon Delight' spill out of a raised, circular planter.* **Molina caerulea** *'Variegata' fills an antique iron urn and adds another vertical element.*

RIGHT *Comfortable patio furniture is a must. Low planters of* **Echeveria** *and a big pot of the dark-leaved* **Cimicifuga simplex** *'Hillside Black Beauty' are all there is room for on a small raised patio.*

I N THE TEN YEAR INTERVAL BETWEEN WRITING THE LETTER AND receiving that phone call, there had been no contact between us. I didn't even know his name. I had met my partner Brent, and we had a tiny but perfect little seven-hundred-square-foot shingle cottage in one of the city's less glamorous areas. The exodus from Hong Kong was hitting Vancouver hard. Countless older homes and many mansions were razed to make way for "International Style" monster homes. I knew what I had to do.

Dr. Kania said to come over right away. I asked if I could bring my "brother" — I didn't want to blow this opportunity to see inside the house! I will never forget ringing the doorbell, expecting "Max," or at least Harvey Korman dressed as "Max," to open the door. Instead, a very short Alfred Hitchcock type greeted us, with a badly-wigged woman peering over his shoulder. The first thing he said to me was, "I've spent ten years checking you out. You are the only person I will sell my house to."

To make a long story short, he was serious. He considered me an "artist" and he believed his house, his pride and joy, would be in safe hands. He was almost ninety, and the time to pass it on had come. Luckily, I had a great bank manager! I drove him past the house and he said "Don't worry." Brent and I managed to finally sell our tiny cottage, skip several steps and move into a house ten times bigger. The past fifteen years have been spent working on the house and the garden, trying to put beauty everywhere.

FACING PAGE *Abutilon* 'Huntington Pink' and *Hedera helix* 'Goldheart' *follow the curves of a garden wall.* **Stipa arundinacea** *froths about, while succulents in a shallow moss-and-chicken-wire nest adorn the top of the wall. A peel-and-stick waterproof membrane went down first, with everything else resting on top.*

MY STYLE OF GARDENING OWES A LOT TO THIS HOUSE. THE whole look of the place became much more dramatic when we painted it a rich salmon. I tried thirteen colors, and remember a neighbour saying "You're not *really* painting it that color, are you?" After being white for nearly sixty years, it was a dramatic change. Now everyone loves it. It has mellowed, and I like the mottled effect of algae, sun and shadows on its rich surfaces. Plants pop out against my peachy walls.

The garden is actually very small. It encircles the house, and a path of cast-concrete pavers that look like mellow Yorkstone allows you to see it all without much effort. Beds are accessible from this path, and pots decorate the odd set of steps and two sunny terraces. I splurged on a very large hot tub/plunge pool, but it too is beautiful.

Dealing with such a major plant addiction has made me ruthless in tearing things out. There is actually very little still here of what Dr. Kania planted. Two groups of enormous **Chamaecyparis x lawsoniana** date back to when the house was built; they are now at least seventy feet tall, and break the wind from the bay below. My already warm garden is a microclimate because of them. I also kept a huge fig tree, **Ficus carica**, that produces delicious figs every August. A weeping birch, **Betula pendula** 'Youngii', got to stay only because it creates privacy.

I view the rest of the garden as a big plaything. Like a child, I wander outside with no mission on my mind, then suddenly and randomly find something to do. Something to play with. I rearrange pots, cut back **Eryngiums** and **Verbascums**, or dig out a peony that doesn't bloom. I garden.

FACING PAGE *I expected it to succumb to our regular but light frosts, but an Australian tree fern, **Alsophila australis**, has survived year round in a sheltered corner. An antique garden chair competes for pattern against its magnificent fronds.*

CREATING A "MEDITERRANEAN STYLE" GARDEN TO GO WITH MY house's architecture hasn't stopped me from indulging in woodland plants. I love them, too. I unknowingly created a shady walk between my house and the neighbors. Here I grow many jewels that would look inappropriate out front in my "burglarproof" border of yuccas and other spiky plants. I am trying to collect as many forms of hart's tongue fern, **Phyllitus scolopendrium**, as possible. This evergreen has undivided leaves (fronds) that come in a number of forms. My favorite is totally ruffled, like a tacky tuxedo shirt. I adore these ferns so much, I had a sofa upholstered in botanically accurate fern fabric! No one can sit on it.

I use my garden as a laboratory, to see what new trends I can come up with for my nursery. Daylilies, succulents and ways to integrate them artistically seem to be where I am now. Such odd bed-fellows make it quite a challenge. And *that* is exactly what I need.

Casa Triangulo

When I come home I often say, "I'd like to see the wizard, please." My partner Brent is the wizard of many things, one of which is cutting up tile and pieces of slate. Our garden benefits immensely from his decorative treatment of all hard surfaces.

CHAPTER 10 *Tastes Like Chicken*

IF THE WORDS "TENDER" AND "SUCCULENT" IMMEDIATELY MAKE you think of chicken, this chapter should change your life. Tender succulents are to today's hippest gardeners what *Canna* and *Colocasia* were five years ago. They are the epicenter of a new botanical quake of creativity. Their ease of culture and fabulous variety of form allow *anyone* to create something fairly amazing their very first try.

My adventures with tender succulents began in the late 1980s, when my partner Brent bought a few flats of surplus *Echeverias* at our local botanical garden's plant sale. They were leftovers from the parks department's elaborate summer bedding schemes, and a real bargain at $5 per *flat!* Since Victorian times, civic crews have used the tight rosettes of *Echeverias* to spell out words and edge formal beds. Although not winter hardy in our mild Pacific Northwest climate, we began using them as garden plants anyway. At first they filled odd empty spaces at the fronts of borders, mixing well with perennial grasses and hot, spiky favorites such as *Eryngium* and *Dierama*. We always made sure to lift them before any real danger of frost, and overwintered them in a heated but cool greenhouse.

PREVIOUS PAGE *Potted succulents really are the treasure trove. Here, bits of coral add stark contrast in an arrangement by my partner, Brent Beattie.*

FACING PAGE *The handmade terra cotta pots from Impruneta, Italy, are perfect for holding a collection of Echeverias. The very dark Echeveria 'Black Prince' contrasts well with a chunk of coral and creates an undersea vision.*

BELOW *A mixed pizza of blooming, completely hardy* **Sempervivum**, *the fabulous-but-tender* **Kalanchoe thyrsiflora** *and a few* **Echeverias**. *The* **Kalanchoe** *takes on a vibrant foliage "tan" the more sun it gets, then completely loses it in the greenhouse each winter. The container is an unusual double-rimmed "ant saucer" from Italy.*

ABOVE *A completed "Echeveria Pizza" in a low clay saucer. Be sure to jam-pack it or it won't look right.*

LEFT *The frilly* **Echeverias** *are mostly unnamed hybrids. They are also the hardest to find outside of California. But isn't that what overhead bins are for on domestic flights?*

LEFT *In this display at Southlands Nursery,* TYLER MERKEL *uses a broken, but still beautiful terra cotta pot by Whichford Pottery. The popular houseplant burro's tail (**Sedum morganianum**) cascades from a created crevice of broken clay.*

BELOW *Tiny terra cotta pots hold tiny **Sempervivums** on my patio. Although they look Italian, these cute "knock-off" pots are made in China.*

RIGHT *If you can't find enough **Echeverias**, use **Sempervivums**, which are widely available and come in many rich colors. They are also very tolerant of extreme winter cold, and thrive in baking summer heat!*

I SOON BEGAN NOTICING MORE UNUSUAL FORMS AND COLORS OF these charming little cuties in the cactus selections at our "big box" stores. Every so often I would rescue an exceptionally blue or mauve *Echeveria* from the dreary tables and add it to our selection. Then I found black ones, wavy ones and one with blistery warts ('Paul Bunyon'). These were too special to place in the open garden and needed to be featured in shallow pots. The "Echeveria Pizza" was born!

Knowing that these Mexican natives like full sun and excellent drainage, we began potting them in shallow containers. Clay saucers are perfect for this, but first need to be drilled to create drain holes. Terra cotta has an appropriate texture for housing succulents, as its natural roughness contrasts well with their crisp smoothness. It is better to plant your pizza tightly right from the start; I butt each root ball up against its neighbor's root ball for a full look. Usually one or two plants are a little bigger or more special than the others: these will be the focal point of the arrangement, and you have to place them as such. Don't place them in the center — that is too obvious and unartistic — but off to one side, for a less "man-made" look. Group supporting plants around and fill any crevices with potting medium.

SUCCULENTS ARE NOT FUSSY ABOUT SOIL. AS LONG AS EXCESS water drains out and the sun shines, they are happy. I like to top dress succulent creations with a small pea gravel. If you look hard enough you will find lovely biscuit-brown gravels for sale; they certainly look better than grey crushed rock. You may want to add non-living accents such as bits of coral or seashells to create an underwater illusion. The resemblance to sea creatures is striking and a bit of a mindbender when well done.

Succulents used as summer ornamentals should be fertilized occasionally. They respond gratefully by plumping up and getting much larger than expected! I water them every few days in hot weather, and once a month I treat them to a liquid feed of 20-20-20 fertilizer at a higher than recommended dose. I put about two heaping tablespoons of this powdered fertilizer in my one-gallon watering can and deliberately sprinkle the entire rosette of leaves and the soil, to feed both foliage and roots. I know that their succulent leaves allow them to survive droughts in the wild, but I have seen them shrivel and lose the will to live when treated like cacti. They *love* moisture as long as it comes — and *goes*.

FACING PAGE *Seashells deliberately pick up the burgundy tones of this* **Sempervivum**. *Notice that the gravel mulch is a pleasant biscuit brown, not grey or, worst of all, white!*

LEFT By late summer, my planters are bursting but happy. The icy "blue chalk sticks," **Senecio mandraliscae**, adds textural interest to this otherwise "one topping" pizza. An occasional dousing with 20-20-20 fertilizer in the water creates lush growth.

BELOW **Aeonium arboretum** 'Schwarzkopf', a frilly **Echeveria** hybrid.

THE TREND OF GARDENING WITH MASSES OF NON-HARDY succulents is limited by the fear of winter. What do you do with them then? They are too beautiful to be considered disposable. All they need is bright light and an above-freezing windowsill to hang in there until spring. Lack of light in winter will result in stretched growth and very unattractive plants. Lower leaves will turn yellow, then papery and need constant removal. If you cannot provide a very bright location for winter storage of your succulents, give them to someone who can, or set up a grow light in the basement or an unused area. Keep the plants very close to the tubes if these are fluorescent, and watch for stretching.

Gardeners with hundreds of *Echeverias* (they multiply like rabbits!) stash them in plastic flats, not pots. At my house, I call this "Operation Echeveria Lift." Around Halloween, helpers from my nursery come with our big truck and we begin scooping them up with our bare hands. We place them tightly beside each other in plastic nursery flats and spend the next month cleaning them up. We check for insect grubs, slugs and rot, then group the plants by variety and place them, root ball and all, in flats. They spend the winter in semi-hibernation in a barely heated but bright green-house. They receive much less water (maybe once a week) and are allowed to rest.

Around March 1, I begin fertilizing again. A liquid feed of 20-20-20 at half my usual strength wakes them up. The increased light that spring brings really turns these plants on! Struggling specimens suddenly perk up and look happy. Once all danger of frost has passed, I place the flats of *Echeverias* out in the sun to "harden off" for a month or so. This direct sun brings out the subtle coloring and individuality of each variety. Then it is time to play!

CHAPTER 11 *Investment Potting*

MOST GARDENERS WOULD NEVER PUT THE WORDS "INVESTMENT" and "potting" together. But potting has a lot more in common with banking than you might think. Your pots and containers should pay an *aesthetic dividend,* as well as contain your plants. In other words, buy some good pots!

I find I am inspired by my containers themselves. I once lugged home an antique cast iron *jardinière* from the Paris flea market, and I am not about to fill it with meaningless impatiens; its weathered, metallic patina deserves better. The tiny celadon-green leaves of **Hebe** 'Quicksilver' and a dark apricot **Diascia** 'Coral Belle' made a lovely combination for this pot. Another year I filled it with the coppery foliage of **Haloragis erecta** 'Wellington Bronze'; this easy-from-seed New Zealand weed behaved well for me, though I've heard it is a terrible self-sower elsewhere.

For an increasing number of people, container gardening is their only choice. Housing prices only go up and balconies keep getting smaller. What used to be the size of a bank vault is now more like a safety deposit box. All the more reason to use it wisely. Your choice of containers is an *aesthetic milestone.* Think of it as a major hurdle that will decide whether or not you are even in the race.

PREVIOUS PAGE *Hedera helix* 'Buttercup' *marries this aged olive jar to its bed of* Hakonechloa macra *'Aureola' grass at* CHANTICLEER GARDENS *in* WAYNE, PENNSYLVANIA. *By keeping the ivy under control, the beauty of the jar is not lost. It looks like it has always been there.*

LEFT *Diascia* 'Blackthorn Apricot' fills a French antique iron planter on my patio. Behind it, the dark spears of *Eucomis* 'Sparkling Burgundy' rise. A particularly fine Italian terra cotta pot is deliberately left without trailing plants, as I want to appreciate its decorative detail.

BELOW A handmade terra cotta olive oil jar and column from Impruneta, Italy, serves as sculpture in my own garden. I cut down an evergreen magnolia tree to make room for them, and don't regret the decision. *Hosta* 'Sum and Substance' and *Dienanthe bifida* play back-up roles and allow the jar to star. *Parthenocissus quinquefolia* 'Engelmannii' forms a delicate tracery and adds interest to the background wall.

RIGHT *Fuchsia* 'Autumnale', *Cuphea ignea* and *Setcreasea purpurea* spill and *Eucomis* 'Sparkling Burgundy' rises from a pot on my patio. I like to assemble plants for their foliage value rather than any flowers they may produce.

In the VANCOUVER, B.C., *garden of* MAUREEN LUNN, *custom-made bronze planters hold a different and dazzling display each year. Their wide, open shape allows for a mounding of soil and a non-flat final composition of pure artistry. Plenty of succulents mix with a touch of purple from* **Setcreasea purpurea** *and* **Sedum** *'Bertram Anderson'. Silvery* **Santolina chamaecyparissus** *and lime green* **Sedum makinoi** *liven things up in one planter, perched high over a ravine.*

*Echeveria Pizzas — once you make one, it is hard to stop. The very dark **Echeveria** 'Black Prince' combines with a few spiral seashells and a touch of burro's tail (**Sedum morganianum**) in an Italian "ant saucer."*

GARDENING IN CONTAINERS IS ANOTHER FORM OF SELF-expression. Like painting or taking a pottery class, you are revealing things about yourself every time you put two plants together. Psychiatrists study people's doodles, so what do your containers say about you? Does a giant concrete boot *and* a plastic swan planter suggest arrested development or cruelty to animals? I have been tempted to knock on strangers' doors and ask them if they even knew they had a hanging basket out front. If so, why is it dead?

The ship has literally come in for small space gardeners. Containers of containers from Vietnam, the Philippines and China are flooding all markets with great-looking, inexpensive glazed pots. Available in many colors, some of the best looking ones are also dirt cheap. I particularly like the tawny brown and mustardy tones. These solid, neutral colors often have a matte or even rough finish that appears almost unglazed. They combine particularly well with simple plantings of grasses: tufts of **Nassella** (formerly **Stipa**) **tenuissima**, sugary brown **Carex flagellifera** and the dried blood-red **Uncinia rubra** are enough on their own. Such simple pots look best in groups of three to five, and one tipped on its side and half-buried looks great!

There is something mesmerizing about blue glazed pots. I think we simply don't get enough blue in our lives. There is a true short-age of blue flowers in the world, so we have to compensate. Cobalt glazed pots deliver a throbbing fix — they make nearby foliage appear more glaucous, and succulents housed in them look icy and cool. When working with strongly colored containers, limit yourself to just one part of the spectrum. Additional pots have to be neutral, terra cotta or something similar. A grouping of containers should look like a gallery exhibit, not a garage sale.

LEFT *Little Miss Muffet?
Actually it's a happy pot of*
Origanum *'Barbara Tingey'.
Very special and favorite plants
are often shown to best advantage on their own. This sun-
lover has proven to be much
hardier than I thought, and
now spends all year outdoors.*

BELOW **Oxalis spiralis** *ssp.*
vulcanicola *cascades from a
mixed pot in* ROGER RAICHE *and*
DAVID M^cCRORY'S *garden. This
recent introduction produces
coppery-tinged new growth that
fades to shades of lime. Notice
the rock, which adds greatly to
the plant composition.*

GLAZED POTS ARE RARELY FROSTPROOF AND NEED TO BE OVER-wintered inside. Glazes trap water and will often crack or chip from cold. Cold-climate gardeners should not risk losing containers by leaving them outside all winter, even filled with soil. Gardeners in milder areas can keep on using their pots in winter and usually plant them seasonally. I own several hand-made Italian terra cotta pots from the famous Impruneta potteries. For centuries, this small town near Florence has produced the most beautiful clay pots in the world. Family-owned businesses hand press a particularly iron-rich local clay into molds. After firing, this clay turns a distinctive peachy-rose shade that is instantly recognizable as an "Impruneta pot." Their high iron content and surprisingly heavy weight make these pots more frostproof than other clay pots. And their design and ornamentation are so timeless that any plant benefits aesthetically just by association.

By purchasing a few "investment pots," you automatically raise the bar. What you put in them now matters. They become receptacles for botanical treasure, no longer utilitarian vessels or coffins of misery. Owning a few "important" pots also makes plant shopping more fun. Now you will want to evaluate whether or not a plant is *worthy*. You establish a balance between plant and container, and in doing so create a Jewel Box Garden.

In VICTORIA, B.C., VALERIE MURRAY *clusters pots of sun-lovers together. The bronze blades of New Zealand flax* (**Phormium tenax** *'Atropurpureum') gain some additional height by being grown out of the ground. A plain Asian pot keeps the focus on the plant material.*

THERE ARE ENDLESS OPTIONS WHEN CHOOSING A CONTAINER theme. But make plastic your last resort: it announces budget constraints loudly. For the same outlay, you can easily find alternatives in wood, clay or metal. Zinc has become popular. Its contemporary, smooth shapes are perfect for holding "modern-looking" foliage plants such as **Elegia capensis, Chondropetalum, Equisetum** and grasses. The almost black rosettes of **Aeonium arboretum** 'Schwarzkopf' always arouse plant lust and do well outside in pots. Don't obsess over "hardy/not hardy" or you won't have any fun and certainly won't be creative. Most of the fun stuff is not hardy except in the mildest areas, so get over it! For decades gardeners have been brainwashed into planting "annuals" as dictated by the dullest nursery conglomerates possible. Luckily, there is a plant resistance movement. Come, join us!

After a while, some plants become special to you. In the world of Jewel Box Gardening, these are your estate jewels. If there was a fire, you would grab them while your CDs and clothing burned. I once carried three **Agave americana** 'Mediopicta' plants across North America in the overhead bins on airplanes. I told fellow passengers they were wedding bouquets, and nobody squashed them! They are the Tiffany of agaves, and I still treasure them. Each leaf has a pure white stripe down its center and the whole plant has a tailored, geometric growth habit. I know not to mix them with "lesser jewels" and allow them to star in their own pots on my terrace.

FACING PAGE *Dark leaves of* **Dahlia** *'Bishop of Llandaff' and* **Aeonium arboreum** *'Schwarzkopf' frame an exciting tableau in* VALERIE MURRAY'S *garden. The duo of a well-placed blue bowling ball and a pottery vase makes a perfect focal point.*

MY GOOD FRIEND HELEN DILLON, A PLANTSWOMAN FROM Dublin, Ireland, refers to her favorite plants as "tots." I suspect they know it: every temperamental treasure thrives for her. Good gardeners establish a rapport with their plants, and container plants need this the most. *They depend on you* — I think this is an unwritten rule of gardening. By isolating a plant from contact with the earth itself, you are taking on the responsibility for its welfare. Container gardening leaves less to chance — you really are in charge.

Much depends on what you use for "soil" in your pots. Most packaged "soil" is largely peat and a horrible fraud. I would never use it as is. Buy some if you must, but amend it liberally with actual organic matter. Composted manures are easily available: I like well-rotted steer manure and aged mushroom manure. I create a more "living soil" for my pots by mixing these at a proportion of about one third each! That means that for every bag of "potting soil," I blend in a similarly sized bag of each of these two manures. I end up with a yummy, friable, water-holding mix that my container plants love. I also find it unnecessary to change container soil. Summer annuals receive monthly applications of 20-20-20 delivered by watering can. This gives them a quick fix that produces lush growth and more bloom.

A punch of color in MARNIE MCNEILL'S VICTORIA, B.C., *garden comes not from plants, but from an empty pot. This unusual shade of teal blue combines well with neighboring cupid's dart (**Catananche caerulea**) and the straw-yellow buttons of **Santolina chamaecyparissus**.*

D RAINAGE IS AN IMPORTANT ASPECT OF CONTAINER GARDENING. Plants really can drown, and excess water must escape from all pots except water gardens. If you *must* use saucers, raise your pots up out of them by filling them first with gravel. This not only looks better, but allows air to flow in and out of your soil. Roots needs this. There are exceptions, but most plants do not enjoy sitting in water.

A lot of what you can grow is determined by your light and exposure. Most failures are a result of placing plants in inhospitable or completely foreign new homes. They hate it, and die. Shop according to what you have to offer at home. Is it a baking-hot rooftop or a shady balcony? Do some research and find out where a plant came from. Plants that evolved in South Africa will probably like your blazing deck; Japanese woodland ferns will not. Real gardeners always make the effort to satisfy a plant's genetic programming.

By selecting inspiring containers and trying exciting, off-beat plants, *you have won half the battle*. Throw in the secret ingredient — commitment — or nothing much else is going to happen.

FACING PAGE *The apple-green umbels of* **Angelica pachycarpa** *anchor an enormous jar in* ROGER RAICHE *and* DAVID M^cCRORY'S *old garden in* BERKELEY. *Why is scale a toy most seem afraid to play with?*

CHAPTER 12 *Stirring Up Ghosts*

I LIKE THE CONCEPT OF TRYING TO MAKE GARDENING A LITTLE more spiritual. I do my best thinking while weeding, away from life's distractions. I know I am more vulnerable while gardening — my defenses disappear. Therapists now use gardening as medication, whereas we have always administered our own doses.

In this doped-up state of gardening euphoria, it is possible to become very melancholy. This is when we are most creative. Think of all great painters, and what they painted *from*. Creativity comes from adversity, not from art school. Maybe your garden isn't exciting because you haven't suffered. What is interesting about any landscape plan? It is time to look deeper and find the door to your well of creativity. *Access the scary side of your personality.* I like listening to *very* sad songs by Jane Olivor, Helen Schneider or Jackson Browne. I absorb the lyrics, to be rehashed later in my mind as I plant. I feel lucky, and blessed that I have not had to go through most of what they sing about. For me, this audio fertilizer is a form of sensitization. My mind has now tuned in to a higher channel, where like spirits dwell.

The results are certainly better than mindless "landscaping." One only has to drive by any new housing complex or commercial project to see a lack of spiritual connection to plants. Like abandoned puppies, plants are stranded in mass graveyards. For true gardeners, it is our personal bond and actual concern for their welfare that keeps our plants happy, if not healthy.

PREVIOUS PAGE *Kiss the pretty picture? I don't think so. Some life force seems to inhabit the dark waters of an amazing ruin in these unsettling carved marble heads by* BERKELEY, CALIFORNIA, *artist* MARCIA DONAHUE. *A fairly recent addition to Chanticleer Gardens in Wayne, Pennsylvania, this gutsy folly stands alone in public or private horticulture. For now.*

LEFT *Mysteriously placed in* ROGER RAICHE's *former garden in* BERKELEY, CALIFORNIA, *this ceramic book stopped me in my tracks. That is the sign of good garden ornament.*

BELOW *In her own* CALIFORNIA *garden,* MARCIA DONAHUE's *carved stone leaves soften the fall of an artistic accident. A sad and broken little man lies at the feet of the sculpture* **Big Beauty**, *as art imitates life once again.*

BELOW *The insect-eating pitcher plant,* **Sarracenia rubra**, *waits silently while ceramic slugs frolic around a carved granite skull. It could only happen at Marcia's.*

ABOVE *Protected by her bamboo fortress, sleeping beauty (a non-Disney version) rests in* MARCIA DONAHUE'S *private theme park in* BERKELEY, CALIFORNIA.

LEFT **Cedrus atlantica glauca** *'Pendula' softens copper entry doors in* CEVAN FORRISTT'S SAN JOSE, CALIFORNIA, *garden. Its verdigris needles echo in a cryptic message while an intimidating stone head from Thailand keeps the timid at bay.*

LEFT *At Lotusland,* GANNA WALSKA'S *realized dream in* MONTECITO, CALIFORNIA, **Euphorbia ingens** *tries to protect the house from visitors. Forming a terrifying curtain, this plant fills an important role, and I am sure Ms. Walska's spirit directs its every move. Golden barrel cactus (**Echinocactus grusonii**) acts as ground cover.*

BELOW **Echeveria elegans** *surrounds a mysterious hole in* BOB CLARK'S OAKLAND, CALIFORNIA, *garden. I like to think of this as a portal — is something coming out, or do we go in?*

WHITE CALLA LILIES (*Zantedeschia aethiopica*) HAVE AN intrinsic sadness to them, and many people avoid them. I think they are the stars of the arum family and at their best close to a water feature. Bearded iris (**Iris germanica** hybrids) come in the most amazing, hypnotic colors. I grow them in odd shades of brown, near-black and rust. They are happy in full sun and seem to like no competition. Keep them unshadowed by neighboring perennials and replant the rhizome tips often. I always place a handful of bone meal under each rhizome when replanting. This group of plants is unfairly snubbed by nearly all gardeners. No other genus contains such magical colors and impossible beauty.

Other "forgotten" groups of plants, botanical ghosts, include dianthus, **Primula auricula**, ranunculus and chrysanthemums. At some point, these and many more families of plants were enormously popular. Entire societies and exhibitions were devoted to them. Centuries before the present age of DVD and video, collectors in England built "Auricula Theatres" onto their homes. Here they would stage their prized collection of primulas. Are we de-evolving?

RIGHT *Allium christophii* always dries perfectly in situ. Here it is surrounded by the extra-lovely cut-silver foliage of *Centaurea gymnocarpa* in the late STEVE ANTONOW'S SEATTLE garden.

ABOVE *In* ROGER RAICHE *and* DAVID McRORY'S *former* BERKELEY, CALIFORNIA, *garden, it is the bright blue painted window trim, not the plants, that matches the glazed decorative objects. This bonus color intensifies the scene, which otherwise belongs to a strange New Zealand native,* **Pseudopanax ferox**. *Trying hard to look dead, its jagged juvenile leaves feel like plastic and emerge in a terminal blob of clear goo!*

RIGHT *The deciduous* **Catalpa bignonioides** *'Aurea' forms a living sculpture in* LINDA COCHRAN'S *garden near* SEATTLE. *Notice the way a hint of color on the pottery vessel ties it to the color-washed concrete wall.*

170

I HAVE NOTICED A SWITCH IN GARDENING, FROM "PRETTY" TO WHAT I call "The New Ugly." I find this fascinating and very, very attractive. In gardening, *ugly has been redefined* by brilliant plantsmen and -women who get absolutely no thrill from trying to make a pretty picture. By increasing the dosage of all that is weird and unexpected, these thrillseekers are creating powerful, unforgettable experiences. What was garden ornament has become *garden incident*. Adding a few lightning rods is bound to attract bonus energy to your garden.

Certain plants have the added feature of an "afterlife" — they are still of ornamental value when dead. Poppy pods appear sinister. The giant biennial thistle (***Onopordon acanthium***) dries in situ, turning into an eight-foot silvery nightmare of razor blades by July. Of the alliums, my favorite is ***Allium schubertii***. With its 18-inch sparklers atop 14-inch stems, this botanical wonder dries perfectly. ***Allium christophii*** is more accessible but far less spectacular. ***Cardiocrinum giganteum*** produces fabulous stalks of white "lilies," each with a plum-red blotch in the throat. The 10-foot stalks dry perfectly and look like something left behind by Tiki warriors.

Even though it is not reliably hardy outdoors for me in winter, I grow the very odd-looking ***Pseudopanax ferox*** in a pot. This New Zealand native has a fascinating, dead appearance. Its very sculptural, lizard-textured leaves feel like plastic strips of bumps and notches. A dreary army green, they clasp the beanpole-like stem and hang downward. Every so often there is a "birthing" at the top and an amazing clear goo containing a new batch of baby leaves emerges. In its windy native climate, this gel allows the new foliage to photosynthesize without dessicating!

LEFT *A ceramic sculpture of a crow by artist Katherine MacLean adds tension to* JOHN RAMSAY's *garden in* VANCOUVER, B.C. *Black accents reinforce the message that in this garden, nature meets art dealer. Designed by John Minty as an urban refuge and an extension of the house itself, this small garden succeeds as both.*

BELOW *More unsettling than cute, a baby doll head in a wreath of birch twigs "welcomes" visitors at* SHARON OSMOND's *garden gate. I much prefer this to a "Welcome Duck" as a clue to what might lie within!*

Envision your garden as a receiving dish for positive energy. You don't have to tell everyone about it, but try it in secret. Wouldn't you tend an area more lovingly if your favorite pet was buried there? Extend emotional reactions to include your plants. I always tell my **Hemerocallis** 'Elusive Dream' that it's my favorite. That daylily outperforms all my others, and I have *lots* of them. Talking to plants doesn't seem so crazy if you know you are getting a reply.

Not everyone will be able to use a garden in this way. Actually, very few people do, and it shows. Just go for a drive.

In my life, many of the crinkliest eyes (always a good sign) ended up blind and dying of AIDS. This included some of the very best gardeners on the planet. I am simply unwilling to lose contact with them, and my only hope is through plants themselves. I have no proof it works, but my green thumb practically gives off sparks when I remember, "Drake gave me this plant," or "This was Gerald's **Rodgersia**."

The very '90s term "cocooning" sounds all warm and fuzzy, but the terrorist attacks of 9/11 awakened the desire in *everyone* for a safe haven. Those of us who have gardens use them as ongoing therapy. As the world gets scarier, our sessions are longer and we schedule them more often. The sensitive gardener's garden is looking better than ever!

FACING PAGE *The dark foliage of* **Cimicifuga simplex** *'Brunette' brushes against an antique Asian shrine in my garden. Only used on rare occasions, and more for garden lighting than worship, I'm sure it doesn't hurt to light this candle …*

Abutilon 'Huntington Pink', 127
Abutilon 'Melon Delight', 124
Abutilon spp., 92
Acer palmatum, 117
Acorus gramineus 'Ogon', 16
Aegopodium podagraria 'Variegatum', 91
Aeonium arboretum 'Schwarzkopf', 52, 142, 156
Agapanthus spp., 35
Agave americana 'Mediopicta', 38, 108
Agave americana 'Variegata', 33
Agave parryi, 54
Agropyron magellanicum, 55
Alchemilla mollis, 63
Allium christophii, 171
Allium schubertii, 122
Aloe polyphylla, 48
Alsophila australis, 16, 26, 128
Anemone nemorosa 'Allenii', 70
Angelica pachycarpa, 160
Aralia elata 'Aureavariegata', 41
Arthropodium candidum, 64
Asarum splendens, 63
Astelia chathamica, 9
Athyrium filix-femina 'Frizelliae', 63
Ballotta pseudodictamnus, 124
Beta vulgaris 'Bright Lights', 94
Brunnera 'Jack Frost', 99
Buxus sempervirens 'Suffruticosa', 33
Calceolaria alba, 122
Carex elata 'Bowle's Golden', 74
Carex flagellifera, 36, 122
Catalpa bignonioides 'Aurea', 170
Catananche caerulea, 159
Cedrus atlantica glauca 'Pendula' 166
Centaurea gymnocarpa, 37, 171
Cerinthe major 'Purpurascens', 61, 73, 122
Chamaecyparis lawsoniana, 118, 121
Cimicifuga simplex 'Brunette', 175
Cimicifuga simplex 'Hillside Black Beauty', 125
Coleus 'Coral Glo', 92, 96
Coleus 'Tilt a Whirl', 88
Coleus spp., 36
Colocasia antiquorum 'Illustris', 100
Colocasia esculenta 'Jet Black Wonder', 37
Cornus controversa 'Variegata', 58
Cortaderia richardii, 12
Corydalis flexuosa 'Purple Leaf', 95
Cryptocereus spp., 55
Cuphea ignea, 147
Cyathea medullaris, 16
Cyclamen hederifolium 'Bowle's Apollo group', 66

Dahlia 'Bednall Beauty', 91
Dahlia 'Bishop of Llandaff', 156
Dahlia 'Ellen Houston', 91
Deinanthe caerulea, 69
Diascia 'Blackthorn Apricot', 147
Dicentra 'Snowflakes', 77
Dienanthe bifida, 147
Echeveria 'Black Prince', 135, 150
Echeveria elegans, 168
Echeveria spp., 48, 61, 73, 111, 125, 135, 136, 137, 150
Echinocactus grusonii, 168
Ensete ventricosum 'Maurelii', 26, 43
Eucomis 'Sparkling Burgundy', 147
Euphorbia characias 'Wulfenii', 118, 121
Euphorbia ingens, 168
Festuca 'Golden Toupee', 99
Fuchsia 'Autumnale', 147
Fuchsia 'Baby Chang', 96
Fuchsia 'Firecracker', 36
Fuchsia 'Gartenmeister Bohnstedt', 96
Fuchsia 'Genii', 124
Furcraea gigantea 'Striata', 37
Fuschia magellanica 'Molinae', 84
Geranium maderense, 110
Gingko biloba, 93
Hakonechloa macra 'Aureola', 12, 16, 91, 98, 144
Hamamelis 'Jelena', 78
Hedera canariensis 'Variegata', 16
Hedera helix 'Buttercup', 144
Hedera helix 'Goldheart', 127
Helleborus x orientalis, 33
Hemerocallis 'Bela Lugosi', 51
Hemerocallis 'Ed Brown', 70
Hemerocallis 'Forbidden Desires', 41
Hemerocallis 'Lord of Lightning', 41
Hemerocallis 'Pandora's Box', 11
Hemerocallis 'Pizza Crust', 122
Hemerocallis 'Scott Fox', 122
Hemerocallis 'Sedona', 52
Hosta 'Gold Standard', 63, 91, 98
Hosta 'Halcyon', 98
Hosta 'Sagae', 94
Hosta 'Sum and Substance', 147
Ipomoea batatas 'Blackie', 36
Kalanchoe thyrsiflora, 101, 137
Lilium 'Peach Butterflies', 11
Lophomyrtus x ralphii 'Sundae', 9
Loropetalum chinense 'Razzleberry', 9
Lysimachia nummularia 'Aurea', 95
Magnolia 'Forrest's Pink', 118, 121

Mertensia simplicissima, 55, 74
Mollina caerulea 'Variegata', 124
Nassella tennissima, 11
Oncidium spp., 26
Origanum 'Barbara Tingey', 57, 152
Oxalis spiralis ssp. vulcanicola, 153
Parthenocissus quinquefolia 'Engelmannii', 147
Phlomis fruticosa, 11
Phormium 'Sundowner', 50, 61, 73, 92
Phormium tenax 'Atropurpureum', 155
Phormium tenax, 35
Phormium spp., 92
Plectranthus 'Troy's Gold', 16
Plectranthus argentatus, 91
Pleioblastus auricomus, 91
Pleioblastus viridistriatus, 91
Podophyllum delavayi, 66
Primula 'Francisca', 95
Pseudopanax ferox, 170
Pyrus salicifolia 'Pendula', 35
Quercus garryana, 86
Ranunculus ficaria, 70
Rhodochiton atrosanguineum, 36
Rosa 'Graham Thomas', 12
Rosa glauca, 110
Sagina sublata 'Aurea', 103
Sambucus nigra 'Pulverulenta', 11
Santolina chamaecyparissus, 149, 159
Sarracenia rubra, 167
Saxifraga fortunei 'Five Color', 64
Saxifraga fortunei 'Miyuki's Purple', 63
Saxifraga fortunei 'Velvet', 64
Sedum x 'Bertram Anderson', 61, 73, 149
Sedum makinoi, 149
Sedum morganianum, 150
Sempervivum spp., 137, 138, 141
Senecio mandraliscae, 142
Senecio rowleyanus, 33, 36, 59, 109
Setcreasea purpurea, 16, 147, 149
Soleirolia soleirolii 'Aurea', 33
Soleirolia soleirolii, 33, 63
Stipa arundinacea, 127
Strobilanthes dyerianus, 36
Symphytum uplandicum 'Variegatum', 70
Tillandsia xerographica, 38
Tillandsia spp., 26
Trachycarpus fortunei, 118, 121, 124
Veratrum nigrum, 79
Wachendorfia thyrsiflora, 12
Yucca recurvifolia, 118, 121